D1444626

Wisdom is more precious than all riches: and nothing which is desired can be compared to her.

Long life is in her right hand: and in her left are riches and honor.

Her ways are pleasant ways and all her paths are peace.

She is a tree of life to those who grasp her; and he is happy who holds her fast.

Prov. 3:15-18

Salesian Missions wishes to extend special thanks and gratitude to our generous poet friends and to the publishers who have given us permission to reprint material included in this book. Every effort has been made to give proper acknowledgments. Any omissions or errors are deeply regretted, and the publisher, upon notification, will be pleased to make the necessary corrections in subsequent editions.

First Edition Printed in the U.S.A. by Concord Litho Co., Inc., Concord, New Hampshire 03301-0464

♻ Printed on recycled paper

The Tree of Life

from the
Salesian Collection

Compiled and edited by
Sara Tarascio

Illustrated by
Paul Scully
Frank Massa
and
Russell Bushée

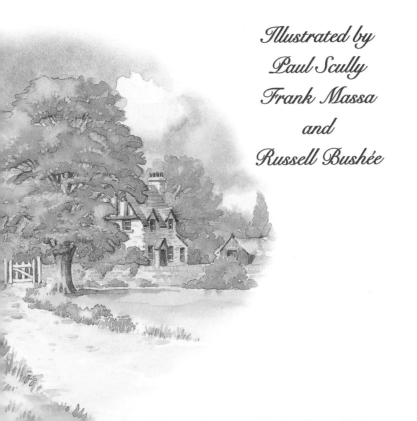

Contents

*O*h the depth of the riches
and wisdom and
knowledge of God! ...
Rom. 11:33

I Know You're There

I know You're there when dawn begins to paint
The skies with color high above my head.
I know You're there when birds begin to sing
In spite of rain, a happy song instead.

I know You're there along the narrow path
That winds beyond the summit of a hill.
And when the twilight falls, 'neath stars above,
Within the silence I have found You still.

I know You're there throughout the busy hours,
I scarce have time to whisper Your sweet Name,
When snowflakes turn the winter world to white,
And autumn burns the hills with her bright flame.

I know You're there when spring peeps through the ground,
And bluebells softly ripple in the wind,
When summer comes and dappled shadows lend
A quiet peace beyond the river's bend.

I know You're there beyond the slightest doubt,
So many times I've felt Your presence when
Doubt blocked the way or when a bridge was out,
And once again You helped me on again.

And through the years when it may well appear
I walk alone and there are none to care,
Dear Lord, what breathless joy to turn around,
...And find You there!

Grace E. Easley

The Home

It need not be a fancy home
To please our latest whim,
The plainest home is beautiful
Where love dwells within.

Where the family lives together
In a warm and caring way,
Who share each other's burdens
And little joys each day.

Where the children grow up happy
Because they know they're loved,
Where God is honored in the home
And prayers are sent above.

It matters not a mansion,
Or a cottage that we own;
Every home is beautiful
Where love's the corner stone.

Kay Hoffman

Chosen Children

In our trust and faith in Jesus
We are safe from earthly harms
And, forever, bless'd with Graces
That are glories of His arms
For we are His chosen children -
He has sanctified by birth -
To be messengers and teachers
Of His ways to live on earth.

It is meant, for us, to serve Him
And do honor to His Name
By performing Christian duties
He has sanctioned or ordained
And we must - as chosen children -
Be disciples to His wills
That promote the loves and mercies
Christianity instills.

Michael Dubina

Blessed is the nation
whose God is the Lord,
the people chosen
as His very own.
Ps. 33:12

Oh, Walk with Me...

Oh, walk with me, my precious Lord;
    Come, walk with me today -
The day is bright; the air is fresh;
    Take my hand and lead the way...

Oh, talk with me, my precious Lord;
    Come, tell me what to say -
The birds are nesting in the trees,
    And the children are at play...

Oh, teach me, oh my precious Lord;
    Come, teach me of Thy love -
I feel Thy warm and tender care
    That comes from heaven above...

Oh, pray with me, my precious Lord;
    Come pray with me tonight -
The stars are twinkling in the sky,
    And it's such a lovely sight...

Oh, sing with me, my precious Lord;
    There's music in the air -
I hear the heaven's happy song,
    And joy is everywhere!

Hope C. Oberhelman

My Quest

I do not seek glory, Lord,
nor do I seek wealth or fame,
and what little good I do,
I do, Lord, in Thy name.

There are lost and lonely souls
who cannot find their way,
but a bit of love and kindness
could help them through each day.

Please let me be Thy messenger,
and all I'll ever ask of Thee -
is to save a little place
in heaven - just for me.

I shall try to earn that place.
Such has always been "my quest,"
I'll do the very best I can,
and to Thee, Lord, leave the rest.

Doris A. Orth

The Little Creek

I sat beside the little creek
and watched the water flow
across the stones and wend its way
to the husky river below.

I sat here in my childhood
with my books and dreams to grow
and all the while the little creek
ran to the river below.

The small stones got more polished,
my books were set aside,
my dreams did not all come true
but the little creek kept its glide.

As I grew older and more mature
one fact I could bestow,
the little creek would always run
and join the river below.

Our life is like the little creek
that travels on and on.
It carries us to a greater end
and we are never really gone.

Florence L. Miller

Abide with Me

Abide with me my Savior,
When clouds Thy dear face hide;
When shadows seem to lengthen,
Oh be Thou by my side.

Abide with me my Savior
And give me sweet repose;
In Thee my soul has blossomed,
From bud to full-blown rose!

Abide with me dear Savior,
And keep my hand in Thine;
That I be in Thee nurtured,
As branch attached to vine!

Abide with me my Savior,
And let me never fear;
What life may hold tomorrow,
As long as Thou art near!

Abide with me my Savior,
That darkling clouds depart;
My strengthening, sturdy fortress,
To be Thy loving heart!

Sancie Earman King

O Lord,
my rock,
my fortress,
my deliverer...
2 Sam. 22:2

13

Evening Prayer

Dear God, what have I done today
To help another on life's way?
Preoccupied, did I not see
Those needs You placed in front of me?

I feel an emptiness tonight
Because I failed to do the right.
I spent my hours selfishly
And now I come on bended knee.

I sought for happiness my way,
But found a joy that did not stay.
Dear God, forgive my waywardness,
My sins to You I now confess.

Tomorrow, Your love I will spread,
And by Your will, I pray be led.
I'll try my best in every way
To make it, God, a better day.

I'll take time for another's need
With thoughtful word and kindly deed;
And then when comes the eventide
Within my heart peace will abide.

Beverly J. Anderson

If we confess our sins,
He is faithful and just
and will forgive us
from all wrongdoing.
1 John 1:9

Surrounded by Beauty

I'm surrounded by beauty
wherever I go.
Both sunrise and sunset
are a wonderful show.

Each season's a treasure,
a sight to behold,
From the roses of summer
to autumn's first gold.

From the lilies of Easter
to winter's first snow,
I'm surrounded by beauty
wherever I go.

Both mountains and valleys
bear witness to me
That God's in control
of all that I see.

From the stars high above
to the oceans below,
I'm surrounded by beauty
wherever I go.

Clay Harrison

The Architect

Do not plan your future,
God knows what to do,
Build your house with the plans
He gives to you!
Do not be afraid, He will lead you on,
He can see the future,
Trust Him with each dawn!
His rock is your foundation,
His corner-stone your shield,
If the root of your faith
Is grounded in Him,
A strong house will be your yield!
Let your four walls
Contain these gems,
A calmness of spirit
And a love for all men!
Root out anguished thoughts,
Let your joy increase,
And the roof of your house,
Shall be made of God's peace!

Anna M. Roos

Blessings!

I've health and home and family...
That's plain for all to see,
I count each as a blessing
...For God's so good to me!
I marvel at each sunset
And sunrise that I see,
I revel in their beauty
...For God's so good to me!

When cooking in the kitchen
Or drifting on the sea,
I have that peaceful feeling
...For God's so good to me!
It's not because I'm worthy
For that could never be...
I'm grateful for His mercy
...For God's so good to me!

Secure within His wisdom
I'll follow faithfully,
By love and peace surrounded
...For God's so good to me!
Now, looking to the future,
Contented I will be,
So long as He is leading
...For God's so good to me!

Anna M. Matthews

The Joys of a Happy Home

May the sun shine in your windows
And reflect its golden rays,
To bring you happy moments
And bright new sunshine days.

May all the love that can unfold
Fill each and every room,
Every day throughout the week -
Each morning, night and noon.

May your doors that open daily
Bring happiness inside,
Along with lasting friendships
That you regard with pride.

May your roof give faithful shelter
Under stars that shine above,
Your walls stand strong and stately,
This house fit like a glove.

May sweet peace and joy abide
Within your chosen place,
Compliments of God on high
Through His endearing grace.

Catherine Janssen Irwin

Wishful Dreams
of Greying Years

Our greying years are seldom kind
To hopes and dreams of heart and mind
For we grow tired - in greying years -
And fill with aches and doubts and fears
But, still, we dare to wish and dream
Of racing winds and wading streams
And chasing joys we used to know
In youthful years - so long ago.

And it is meant that this should be -
As Heaven's gift to you and me -
To bring us smiles, against the truth
Of, once again, re-living youth
For - in such reveries of glee -
Our hearts are young and fancy free
And we are dreamers, Heaven blessed,
To wish and dream in God's caress.

Michael Dubina

*Do not cast me off
in the time of old age;
forsake me not
when my strength
fails me.*
Ps. 71:9

A Change of Color

I walk among the meadows,
grasses deep and shiny green.
Wildflowers paint the landscape,
none so fair I've ever seen.

As I take in all this beauty,
my breath's near taken 'back,
To think of the Creator, all He's made,
there is no lack.

For He can paint the meadows,
wash them clean with heavenly rain,
And He can take a hurting soul
and bind up all its pain.

He can take the vilest life
and cleanse it for His pleasure.
He can take the coldest heart
and warm it beyond measure.

A broken spirit He accepts,
a contrite heart He'll mend
If we'll but give our lives to Him
and all our burdens rend.

He'll paint our lives anew, afresh,
with colors brightly shining.
Our lives once dark, in pain so drear'
will glisten with refining.

Lynda Bryan Davis

*Bless the Lord, O my soul,
and forget not all His benefits.*
Ps. 103:2

Our World Is God's

The universe belongs to God
And that includes our earth,
With every form of life there is,
Whatever be its worth,
The lion and the smallest flea,
Each baby that is born,
The flowers in a garden and
The fields of wheat and corn.
Whatever living thing there is,
Almighty God created,
And only as it serves His will,
Can it be compensated.
Our plants and fish and animals,
Have nothing now to fear,
Because they have no way to voice
Or show they are sincere,
But we, as human beings with
A will that is our own,
Must honor His commandments as
We bow before His throne.

James J. Metcalfe

Be Alone
with Jesus

God directs us in His Word
To spend time alone in prayer.
When we sincerely call His name,
He's always waiting there,
Ready to listen to our plea
And to comfort our broken heart.
He gives us guidance for each task,
Whenever we draw apart
From others and our daily cares,
And give Him our rapt attention.
He frees us from our worries,
And eases all pent-up tension.
He soothes each hurt we suffer
With His healing balm.
He anoints us with His oil of love,
And leaves us serene and calm.

Fern Hanlin Coberly

I Give Thanks

I give thanks for Autumn days
And for Springtime's flower displays;
Mist that rises in the early morn -
And a sun filled day new-born.

Murmuring brooks and streams that flow
Shining stars and bright moon-glow,
Shelter from a frightening storm -
A happy home to keep me warm.

Loved ones ever close to me,
Friends to keep me company;
Twilight time that's all aglow -
Memories that overflow.

I give thanks that I reside
In the American countryside;
For happiness as twilight nears -
As I enfold life's souvenirs.

Nora M. Bozeman

Give thanks
to the Lord,
call upon His name,
make known among
the people, His deeds.
1 Chr. 16:8

*W*ithout the Way there is no going;
Without the Truth there is no knowing;
Without the Life there is no living.

Thomas à Kempis

Intangibles

The gift of love is never measured
In a monetary way,
For it is only manifested
In the actions we display.

The time we spend with children
Giving guidance, tender care,
Teaching, praising and up-lifting,
and just by being there.

The helping hands we offer,
Small things we do to please,
These are the precious treasures
That leave sweet memories.

Our kindness and compassion
To the aged, and infirm,
The giving of our inner selves
Are lasting gifts of endless term.

Words of courage and encouragement,
A hug to show affection,
No diamond, gold or jewel
Can match the glow of love's perfection.

When we touch the hand of strangers
Each time we kneel to pray,
and invite our Lord to enter
We can brighten someone's day.

These intangibles are gifts from God
Priceless love beyond compare
and His love keeps multiplying
If only we would share.

Patience Allison Hartbauer

Faith, Hope and Love...
but the greatest of these is Love.
Cor. 13:13

He Cares for You

When the way seems hard you are called to tread,
When the dark'ning clouds gather overhead,
When despair and grief all about you spread,
Remember: He cares for you.

When your friends cannot help
When you need them most,
When temptations rise as a mighty host,
When you face defeat and the fight seems lost,
Remember: He cares for you.

Then look up to Him, Who the way can show,
He will guide through joy; He will guide through woe;
For His promise holds and it shall be so.
Remember: He cares for you.

Aaron Markuson

*Cast all your cares
upon Him, for He
cares for you.*
1 Peter 5:7

As We Contemplate the Harvest

Once more the rain is falling
like tears from angry clouds,
And the verdant days of summer
are wrapped in charcoal shrouds.
Soon frost will wrap the meadow
in tiny shawls of white,
And the yellow rose of summer
will vanish out of sight.

The aspens now are golden
and the maple's face is red
In the season we call autumn
when humble "thanks" are said.
For truly we are grateful
for the bounty of God's love
As we contemplate the harvest
and praise His name above!

Clay Harrison

Assurance

God knows all that you face today,
He is Compassion and the Way;
He understands your fear, the threat
That looms in circumstance you've met.

He is your shelter in this storm,
Rely on Him and faith is born
To lift you up and set your sail;
To see you safely through the gale.

Fear not! For God is at your side,
Beneath His wings you shall abide;
Recall His love and tender care,
Whisper His name...and He is there.

And as your prayer to Him is made,
Release your fear, be not afraid:
Be quiet...listen...hear Him say,
"My child, I am with you always."

Anna Lee Edwards McAlpin

Everywhere I Look

Everywhere I look I find
Some wondrous handiwork of Thine,
Every single day I see
Some lovely thing You've given me.
My heart almost overflows,
At the sight of velvet rose,
Lacy fern, and birds that sing,
Lord, You give me everything.
As the early morning breeze
Softly stirs through leafy trees,
Comes the dawn all steeped in gold,
More than my two arms can hold.

Silver stars throughout the night,
Purple shadows, pale moonlight
Turn my thoughts again to Thee,
Lord, I fear You're spoiling me.
Everywhere I look I find
Beauty of the richest kind,
Little joys throughout the day
Almost take my breath away.
How very precious I must be,
That You should have such love for me,
And in each cranny, smallest nook
I find You, everywhere I look.

Grace E. Easley

*...The heavens declare the glory of God;
and the firmament showeth His handiwork.*
Ps. 19:1

My Walk
with God

When my busy week has ended
To the country I will trod,
Just to feel the closeness of Him
As I take my walk with God.

Hand in hand from hill to valley
Sweet the smell of fresh turned sod,
Sweeter still my joy and pleasure
As I take my walk with God.

Every creature pays Him homage
Trees and flowers bow and nod
In the presence of their Maker,
As I take my walk with God.

Oh the rapture of this moment
Guided by His staff and rod
Lifted now are all my burdens
As I take my walk with God.

Albert N. Theel

Out
in the
Country

Oh what a pleasure it is to be
Out in the country where life is so free.
Away from the city with its noise and its throng;
Where all is so peaceful and life is a song;
Where the birds sing so sweetly and all is so fair,
And "Old Mother Nature" has scented the air.
Where the deer and the elk and the bear may be seen
And where all is so peaceful, so calm, and serene.
Where, leaving all trouble and worry behind,
And, communing with nature, true peace one may find.
One may angle for trout in a lake or a stream,
Or else one may sit 'neath a tree and just dream,
Where the trees are so tall and the grass is so green
And "The Greatest of Artists" has painted the scene,
With a choice of colors beyond all compare,
Out in the country... how I long to be there!

Out in the country I long to be
Where all is at peace and life is so free.
Is not life a lot like the streams which we view,
Which though often quite peaceful become turbulent too?
Yet where the deer and the elk and the bear can be seen
All is so peaceful, so calm and serene!

Clayton G. Moseley

The Storms of Life

From time to time, the storms of life
must fall upon my way,
I may be bruised and battered
as I stumble through the day,
For the stormy sea may take my boat
and turn it upside down.
By faith I somehow stay afloat
for God won't let me drown.

Sometimes we struggle to survive
according to His will,
But oh, my friend, how good it feels
to climb atop that hill!
Sometimes the wind's not at our back,
but still we run the race.
Sometimes the night is long and black,
but still I seek His face.

We can't avoid the storms of life -
there's no place we can hide,
But faith provides a lighthouse
where angels still abide,
For once the storm has run its course,
a rainbow shall appear -
A promise from the Lord-of-all
that He is always near!

Clay Harrison

Brave Little Ships

We go to sea in ships so brave!
Brave little ships 'gainst wind and tide.
We journey long and ride the deep -
Crossing the ocean wild and wide:
But we sail safe as God's aboard,
Leading our ship and ever guide.

Though waves may come and waves may go -
Our little ship will still sail on.
The night will come and strong winds blow,
All is still well at break of dawn
Because our Savior rides with us:
Staying with us though time be long!

And as our ship breasts the briny deep,
Steering from shoals of sin we see:
What matter ships of some may mock,
We keep our course though longer be.
So sad - their end - a shattered ship!
We, with our Lord, hail victory!

Lynn Fenimore Nuzzi

Then are they glad
because they be quiet:
so He bringeth them
to their desired haven.
Ps. 107:30

33

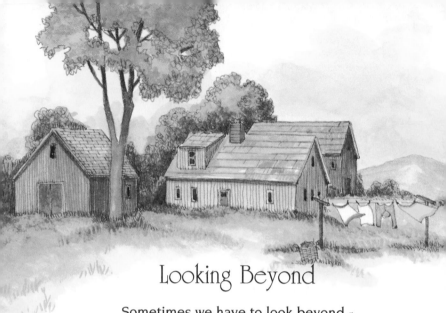

Looking Beyond

Sometimes we have to look beyond -
Beyond so many things
Perhaps the confines of a room,
Beyond our sufferings.

With eyes of faith, we look beyond
The now, with all its fear;
We know a God Who is all-wise
Will one day make things clear.

And so, we look beyond ourselves
To what the Lord can do.
With Him all things are possible.
In time He'll bring us through.

But until then, we must go on
And pray for strength to cope.
Our heart must never lose its song,
Or ever cease to hope.

With gaze that's set beyond the clouds,
We'll keep on pressing on
So thankful that through eyes of faith
We see a brighter dawn!

Beverly J. Anderson

Take Your Joy
from Him

Things will sometimes hurt us,
And people won't be true -
Some will never give to us
The things we think our due!
But whatever happens -
Ne'er let your praises dim;
Raise your voice in thankfulness,
Take your joy from Him!

The sacrifice of thankfulness
Is better than to grieve;
Keeps your heart prepared
The better to receive!
Don't close your heart to others,
Still let the sunshine in;
And while you wait for others
Take your joy from Him!

Lynn Fenimore Nuzzi

Let the
Tea Kettle Whistle

Come share a cup of tea today,
We'll chuckle and dismiss
The greasy dishes, dirty floors,
'Cause housework we won't miss!

Let the tea kettle whistle
For there's a bit of perkiness in the air,
We'll take these "tea-filled" moments
And laugh away each care.

Burdens suddenly become lighter
When sharing a cup of tea or two
With a friend who listens to our woes
And helps to chase away the blues.

Again I say, "Let the tea kettle whistle"
And give thanks for the presence of friends
Who pause from the daily routine to visit -
Praise God for each and every blend!

Linda C. Grazulis

The Sun Is
a Pleasant Sight

I opened the door in the morning
And in came God's beautiful sun.
It was dressed as in gold, a sight to behold;
I saw it was second to none.
It illumined the entire kitchen
With its radiant, all-day smile,
And I saw on its face as I stood there
That it come by to stay for awhile.

As it entered, I greeted it gladly;
Now gone was the dark of the night.
'Twas a pleasure to see its bright beauty;
Oh, it was a sunshiny sight.
It dusted its sunbeams upon me
And stayed with me all day through;
Then it left at the evening sunset
To shine on somebody new.

Loise Pinkerton Fritz

Truly the light is sweet,
and a pleasant thing
it is for the eyes
to behold the sun.
Eccl. 11:7

A Friendly Pet

God must have put a lot of thought
Into my every day,
He sent me such a friendly pet
To run and hide and play.

Her antics of hilarity
Are fun that never end,
And I can count the many ways
She tells me she's my friend.

Our pet was such a tiny one
When first that she arrived,
With softest fur and faintest purr
And much to my surprise

No one would claim this little one
It seem she had no home,
With pleading eyes and kitty sighs
She promised not to roam.

God surely must have sent my way
To keep me company,
This little friend who likes to play
And run and hide from me.

Katherine Smith Matheney

38

What Love Can Do

(Inspired by Genghis Kahn, a cat)

He was battle scarred from head to toe,
But that's the way most tom cats go.
With dirty fur and bloody ear,
He'd run away when we came near.

He tempted fate a time or two
For his nine lives were overdue
And when we found him nearly dead,
He couldn't raise his once proud head.

With time and care he came to know
That he was loved from head to toe,
And soon he learned to love us, too,
When his nine lives were overdue.

How like that cat we run away
And choose a path that leads astray,
Where troubles fall about our head
Till hope and faith are nearly dead.

Then Jesus comes to lift us up,
Restore our strength and fill our cup
That we might see by faith anew
The joy in Him that's overdue!

Clay Harrison

He's Always There

Whatever be our problems,
Whatever be our pain;
Our Father's loving hand is there,
To strengthen and sustain!

For only God can fathom,
Just what we're going through;
And just because He is our God,
There's nothing He can't do!

So when the storm-clouds gather,
And sun does not appear;
We must recall that God's strong hand,
Is always very near!

Sancie Earman King

Cast your care upon the Lord,
He will support you...
Ps. 55:23

Miracle

The Springtime has come,
The Winter is past,
The grip of the cold,
has loosened at last.
Buried deep down,
in the heart of the earth,
The essence of life,
miracle of birth.

The life giving sap,
hears Spring's urgent call,
Faint murm'ring sound
in the trees gaunt and tall.
'Neath the ice of the stream,
swift waters course,
Their strength, increased by
the snow at their source.

Lily S. Thomas

*Truth shall spring
out of the earth and
righteousness shall look
down from Heaven*
Psalm 85:11

41

I Can't Go
Home Again

I really can't go home again.
It was so long ago
When I was young and happy there
So free from care, you know.

I surely had no worries then -
Just lived from day to day
And if I had some cause to cry
That swiftly went away.

The old homestead is stooped with age,
The building's in decay
As though it were a hundred years
Since I had gone away.

I passed by there not long ago
And paused awhile to see
The aged house where I was born
And it looked back at me.

Its window-eyes are dimmed with age,
The roof is sagging and
The old house cannot long survive
Without a helping hand.

The garden where Mom's roses grew
Cannot be found today;
The creek's flat stones that formed our walk
Have long been hauled away.

The wooden fence and posts are gone
As are the hedge and flowers
Which Mother loved and for their care
She toiled so many hours.

The old pond is no longer there
Where livestock used to drink,
Where bullfrogs croaked and turtles swam
And where I went to think.

I really can't go home again
But thoughts of yesteryear
Are vivid in my heart today -
Those mem'ries I hold dear!

Luther Elvis Albright

When Time
Is Short

There's so much left unfinished
when its time for us to go,
like the salmon swimming upstream
against the river's flow.

A poem that's left unwritten;
A story with no end;
A song without the music;
A child without a friend.

We do our best to comprehend
what lies for us in store,
but can't help thinking in the end
there always could be more.

So let us all remember
each day by passing day
to lend a hand to others
and help them on their way.

For God will smile upon us
when our work on earth is done;
the battle finally over ...
the victory finally won!

Karen Taylor

*And let us not grow weary
while doing good,
for in due season
we shall reap
if we do not lose heart.*
Galatians 6:9

44

Final Chance?

The soft and gentle ways of life -
Like Seasons of the year -
Become less full of life's contents
As Winter years draw near,
For Winter years bring aches and ills
That burden life with grief
And, only, in God's Grace of prayer
Is comfort and relief.

But, maybe, it is preordained
That life should wane, this way -
To bring us unto powers of God
And Grace of Judgment Day -
A final chance, for you and me,
To prove, with crying heart,
Our trust and love and Christian faith
In all that He imparts.

Michael Dubina

Winter Wonder

The ermine mantle covering earth
Deftly hides the world once more
As shapes and forms begin to emerge
That have never been seen before.

Branches drip with mother-of-pearl
And diamond frost a rainbow makes
As icy castles and sparkling stars
Are mirrored in shimmering lakes.

And in this transformed magic land
Coated with soft and silent snow,
God's creatures leave a tiny trail
That vanishes into the woods below.

Eva Marie Ippolito

*Thou has set
all the borders
of the earth:
thou hast made
summer and winter.*
Ps. 74:17

All Things
Are Possible

No burden is too heavy,
No cross too great to bear,
If you let God into your life
And let Him with you share.

No mountain is too steep to climb,
Though high that it may be,
If you let God into your life
The summit you will see.

No goals are ever out of sight
That you seek to attain,
As long as God is in your life
You will not strive in vain.

Harold F. Mohn

*"...if you have faith
the size of a mustard seed,
you will say to this mountain
'move from here to there,'
and it will move."*
Matt. 17:20

47

Rest

Lord - give the sun to warm me,
A shower, my soul, to cleanse.
A light breeze to cool - not stormy,
Those hurt - may I make amends.
May my heart and soul be humble
With Your graces, always blessed,
On the road to You, not stumble
Within Your love find rest.

James Joseph Huesgen

When I'm Afraid

Everytime I am afraid,
And shadows dim the way,
When peace seems to elude me,
Even when I pray,
When I am tired and weary,
Struggling through each task,
And I can find no answers,
To the questions that I ask,

Then, more than any other time,
I turn to You for aid,
Trusting You to set aright,
The blunders I have made.
Knowing You will gather up
The pieces from the floor,
Of disillusion, tarnished hopes,
And lovingly restore

Them to their former glory
Without a crack or seam,
And fill the night with peace so I
May close my eyes and dream.
For when I am afraid I know
It's weakness on my part,
Because through every trial I face,
I hold You in my heart.

Dear Lord, please take into account,
This love within my breast,
That burns for You, and know that it
Is all that I possess.

Grace E. Easley

49

Silences

A pouring rain makes melodies
Descending from the sky,
But oh, the quiet sunny days
When clouds move white and high.

The songbirds chirp in early dawn,
Each trills his notes in streams,
But oh, the hours when all is hushed,
And we may dream our dreams.

Some afternoons the trees in winds
Are like soft strummed guitars,
But oh, the stillness of the night
Where we can see the stars.

The rushing wavelets on a lake
Make music's loud release,
But oh, the times of waters calm,
When we may find our peace.

All nature's sounds are beautiful
In water, earth, and air,
But oh, the lovely silences
That call our hearts to prayer.

Jean Hogan Dudley

...a time to keep silence,
and a time to speak.
Eccl. 3:7

Why Didn't I?

If only I could take them back -
the times that I was silent,
though I cared.
Why was my "faith in action"
quite so slack
when others' joys and sorrows needed
to be shared?

There were phone calls that
I could have made,
letters that I might have sent,
countless times I could have prayed,
and precious moments I was given,
better spent.

Forgive me, Lord, for
what I haven't done;
help me become a better image
of Your Son.
Then I won't need to chide myself
and sigh,
"Why didn't I? Why didn't I?"

Barbara A. McDowell

There Is a Gift

There is peace; an inner peace
We cannot understand,
It permeates in a troubled heart
when God is in command.

There is joy; a marvelous joy,
To know we're not alone.
Because the Lord provides the light
into our dark unknown.

There is love; abundant love,
Unfathomed and it's free,
Because our debt for sin was paid
by Christ on Calvary.

There is hope; a blessed hope
Because of God's great love,
He's promised us, through His own Son,
A place prepared above.

There is a faith; a limitless faith,
And yet a grain or two
can move a mountain; heal the sick,
There's nothing it can't do.

These are the gifts; God's matchless gifts
That are so freely given,
Come and partake; experience
Your own sweet taste of heaven.

Margaret E. Taylor

Roll Call

One day you'll bid me come to You,
Forget the earthly cares I knew,
I'll gather roses while I may
To offer You a sweet bouquet.

I'll teach my heart a song to sing
Proclaiming all the joy You bring
To those who kneel to You in prayer
And find Your presence always there.

I wanted You so close to me -
So much I had to learn from Thee -
By learning to love others, too,
Is what has brought me close to You.

Now I look back on all the years
Recall the laughter and the tears
And You were there along the way
To fill my cup for me each day.

Edna Fontaine

*Surely goodness and mercy
shall follow me all the days of my life
and I will dwell in the house of the Lord forever.*
Ps. 23:6

Multiple Blessings

Comfort in times of loneliness,
Blessings in times of sorrow,
Guidance in times of decisions
That we must face tomorrow.

Relief in times of suffering,
Courage in times of fear,
Protection in times of danger,
That may be lurking near.

Peace in a time of turmoil,
Strength in a time of temptation,
Forgiveness in a time of conviction,
Would bring to us such revelation.

Warning in times of indifference,
Deliverance in times we are weak;
Rest in the times we are weary,
These multiple blessings we seek.

Where can we find this guidance?
Why, from our Savior above,
Who always watches over us,
And fills our hearts with love.

Albert N. Theel

Spring Celebration

When I see the golden glory
As the sun begins to rise
And the splendor of the heavens
In the far-off eastern skies -

When I hear the songbirds singing
As the night turns into day,
With fresh dewdrops for their drinking
From the blossoms when it's May -

When the breeze blows soft and gentle
With the scent of sweet perfume
And the hummingbirds are busy
Feasting fast upon the bloom -

Then, with songs and hymns and praises
To creation's Lord and King,
I, with birds and blooms and breezes,
Celebrate the lovely spring.

George R. Kossik

*The flowers
appear on the earth;
the time of the Singing
of birds is come.*
Song 2:12

The Good Shepherd

My Shepherd watches over me
He knows my every need.
Through verdant meadows, pastures green,
surely He doth lead.
All troubled thoughts He gently calms,
my soul He doth restore.
In paths of love and goodness
He guides me evermore.
Though dark the road
Thou art near.
Whither my way,
There's naught to fear,
Thy rod and Thy staff
Comfort me still.
In presence of my enemies
A table Thou dost fill.
With oil anointest Thou my head,
my cup runs goodly o'er.
And surely I shall leave Thy house,
Good Shepherd, nevermore.

Walter Kamens

The Lord is my shepherd;
I shall not want.
Ps. 23:1

In the Garden
of My Soul

A tender heart with words unspoken
Glistening tears like rain-drops fall,
A heart so broken filled with sadness
Is the saddest fate of all.

But there's life beyond the mourning,
There is hope in a tossed storm sea,
There's an answer to each prayer
In our own Gethsemane.

So do your best and keep on trying
Though each mountain high with fear,
God will aid the brokenhearted,
He will dry up every tear.

Rest assured a new tomorrow
Will come through with a brighter hue,
Like the prism in each dew-drop
Making all the wrongs seem new.

Chris Zambernard

*The Lord is close
to the brokenhearted…*
Ps. 34:18

Sometimes

Sometimes the days seem dreary
And weary seems the load,
Sometimes we meet with heartaches
As we travel on life's road.

Sometimes the skies seem darkened
As noonday turns to night,
Sometimes the load seems heavy
With future none too bright.

Sometimes our heart grows weary
With every passing day,
Sometimes a sickness makes us
Upon a bed to lay.

Sometimes does not seem pleasant
As we look upon the sad,
But sunshine follows shadows,
Then, sometime's not so bad.

Sometimes when day seems dreary,
Just remember you can pray.
Sometimes when heartaches gather,
Look to Jesus all the day.

Sometimes when skies seem darkened,
You can look unto the light.
Sometimes when loads seem heavy,
You are walking in Christ's sight.

Sometimes when heart grows weary,
He will understand and care.
Sometimes when sickness gathers,
You have love beyond compare.

Sometimes can be most pleasant
When we look to God above,
And sometimes makes you happy
If you'll look unto His love.

Charles G. Ramsey

My Unfailing
Friend

What a sweet and blessed feeling
When I wake up ev'ry day
Just to feel God's presence near me
Just to know He's there to stay.

Oh, I know I am not worthy
Of His tender love and care,
Still I have His precious promise
That He's with me ev'rywhere.

There will always be the shadows
And we can't escape the night,
Still I know He watches o'er me,
I am always in His sight;

Though the storms may rage around me
Still the Lord will help me stand,
There's a sweet and precious calmness
In the hollow of His hand.

Thomas D. Risk

A Prayer
of Thanksgiving

We thank Thee God for bird on wing,
For love of Thee which solace brings;
For tender moments of each day,
Which special be in their own way!

We thank Thee God for brother man,
Who is the heart of Thine own plan;
For wondrous creatures great and small,
Oh Thou, the Author of us all!

We thank Thee God for moments sweet,
Such as the touch of baby's cheek;
A puppy's frantic wagging tail,
The beauty of a wind-swept sail!

We thank Thee God for time of prayer
In church or home where we prepare
To meet uncertainties of day,
When dark-rimmed clouds are swept away!

We thank Thee God for unearned grace,
The tender warmth of Thine embrace;
For wonders of Thy boundless love
Which brighter be than skies above!

Sancie Earman King

*Give thanks
to the Lord,
for He is good,
His mercy endures forever.*
1 Chr. 16:34

Someone Else's Faults

When judging someone else's faults,
let's stop and list our own.
Compare the notes with who we judge;
we'll see they're not alone.
It's easy to point out mistakes,
that someone else will do,
But as the saying goes, my friend;
"Walk a mile while in their shoes."
It's better to reach out a hand
to help someone in need,
than to stand and point a finger
at someone for a bad deed.
God could have done the same to us,
with His wrath, get everyone!
But instead He washed away our sins
with the blood of His own Son!

George A. Hellard Jr.

And Gently I Will Go

I do not have the courage
to claim with boastful voice
that I am master of my fate
and captain course and choice!

Nor will I heed the challenge
"to rail against the night,
to not go gently toward it
but curse the fading light!"

For I recall another
who meekly bowed His head
and, lamb-like, to the slaughter
permitted He be led!

And no one is a coward
who follows faith's commands
and places life and very soul
in God's almighty hands!

And somewhere waits His Heaven
beyond our tiny sky,
where night's, forever banished,
and only death must die!

John C. Bonser

Christian Giver

Blessed is the Christian Giver
Who will give - with joy of heart -
Gifts of charity and kindness,
God endears and love imparts;
His reward is holy bounty
Of God's tenderness and care
And the Grace of Heaven's blessings
On his daily life and prayer.

Through his gifts of Christian kindness -
That provide another's need -
He is giver and disciple
Of God's mercy, love and creed;
And his soul, of faith and virtue -
Serving God, in Christian ways -
Is a soul of promised glory,
God will Grace on Judgment Day.

Michael Dubina

*Above all
have love among yourselves,
for love covers a multitude of sins.*
1 Peter 4:8

The Thoughtful Things

So many friends and loved ones
Bless our lives each day
In just the little thoughtful things
They often do and say.
A neighbor comes to visit
And brings a word of cheer
It's like a ray of sunshine
Your day had been so drear!
The friend who telephones to ask
How you are getting on,
The thoughtfulness that warms your heart
And lingers all day long.
That special one who came to help
When you were feeling ill,
Her deep concern was comforting,
You think about it still.
So many friends and loved ones
Who help our hearts to smile
In just these little thoughtful ways
That make this life worthwhile.

Kay Hoffman

*This is my commandment,
that you love one another
as I have loved you.*
John 15:12

65

The Power
of Faith

My Lord, my God, my Master,
Whene'er I feel despair,
I turn to You for solace
And always find You there.

Whene'er it seems my trials and woes
Are far too great to bear,
I find new faith and inner strength
In answer to my prayer.

I know the faith that I possess
In You, each newborn day
Will be my ever guiding light,
Each step along the way.

Harold F. Mohn

The Silence
of the Soul

Lord let me know the silence,
The silence of the soul,
That I may hear Your voice
And make Your will my goal.

Let silence then take over
The one and only me,
That charity may enter
And set my spirit free.

For silence did prevail
When earth and sea were made,
When Jesus, Lord, was born
And in the manger laid.

Please lead me to compassion
And so to charity,
And finally through silence
Grant me humility.

Marilyn McNeil de Latour

*The words of the wise
are heard in quiet…*
Eccl. 9:17

Faith

Faith sees what our poor sight cannot,
knows truths which we, at birth, forgot.
Faith reads a script that has no lines
and follows paths unmarked by signs -

Rejects what scornful cynics say
and kneeling in the dark to pray,
perceives that far-off dazzling light
that pierces death's despairing night!

Faith swims against time's ruthless tide;
it leaps across doubt's chasms wide
and, link by link, it welds the chain
that draws us close to God again.

Strong is that chain, Faith will not die
though all our mortal senses try
to hush its brave, persistent voice,
we hear it cry: "fear not - rejoice!"

Rejoice, God will not take away
His promise made to men of clay;
on wings of Faith our souls shall rise
and see forgiveness in His eyes!

John C. Bonser

My Birthday Gift

I gave myself a gift today -
A quiet walk beside the sea.
I watched dawn streak the sky with fire
And heard a gull cry wild and free.

I felt the salt air blowing warm,
Then skipped a stone out in the bay.
And never once did I give thought
To those dark clouds of yesterday.

There was no time to shed a tear
As simple pleasures came my way,
And when at last my day was thru,
I bowed my head and knelt to pray:

Dear Lord, I know You gave this gift
With tender watch from up above.
You gave this day for me to share -
In all I touched, I felt Your love.

Helen M. Motti

*This is the day
the Lord has made.
Let us rejoice and
be glad in it.*
Ps. 118:24

Look Up

Face the sun and each tomorrow
Will grow brighter day by day.
Leave the shadows there behind you
As you travel down life's way.

Greet your friends with God's light shining
In your eyes, your voice, your heart.
Help the weary, unbelievers,
Lend your strength to help them start.

"Believe in Me" is all He's asking.
Have faith and you will see
God is walking there beside you
To change your life and make you free.

Have courage and you will conquer
All the fears that life can hold.
Jesus came and died to save you,
To cleanse your soul and make you whole.

Face each day and share each sorrow
with Him, as you travel down life's road.
Your burdens will seem far lighter
When you share another's load.

Do not hide your light from others,
Show them what God's love can do.
Help the sick, the heavy laden
God will help us if we're true.

Take the time to thank Him often,
Every minute of the day.
I know for I have suffered, fallen;
And my God has shown the way.

Julia Parsons MacDonald

A Quiet Place

Just find a quiet "hiding place,"
A sunny little nook,
Where you'll forget the busy world
With sewing or a book.
Green, potted plant upon the sill,
Kit cat beside your chair.
Now, who's to see you nod your head
While you are napping there?
Hot cup of tea, cold dish of fruit
Will add their special blend,
And you will learn you're not alone,
For Jesus is your friend.
That nook can be a favored place
To think upon the Lord
By praying to Him every day
Or reading from His word.

Norma Childress

Where Did All the Decades Go?

Where did all the decades go?
Time is quickly traveling on.
We're born, we play, we love, we learn
And then, too soon, all this is gone.

Every day we're growing older;
None escape it here on earth.
Like Springtime trees become Autumn leaves,
We all start aging right from birth.

Time is like a railroad train;
A one-way ticket - no turning back.
And the prayer of every passenger
Is to stay securely on the track.

Where did all the decades go?
Just like the twinkling of an eye,
And like a bud becomes a rose,
We blossom forth; still all must die.

But, there's victory over fleeting time,
Anxious moments, fears and strife.
Just trusting God to lead our way
Brings decades of abundant life.

John and Edna Massimilla

*P*raise God, from Whom all blessings flow;
Praise Him, all creatures here below...

Thomas Ken

The Little Blessings

Sometimes the little blessings
Are greatest of them all;
A rose in summer's garden,
A tree so firm and tall,
A bird that lends its music,
One violet growing wild,
The stream along the meadow,
The laughter of a child.

God sends us little blessings
In every newborn day;
The sunrise and the sunset
To cheer us on our way,
A million golden moments
We oft' call commonplace,
Forgetting all the beauty
Of just a smiling face.

The lovely little things in life
However small they be,
So often lend us charms untold,
Embrace us happily.
Do offer thanks to God above
Each time you kneel in prayer,
For all the little blessings
In such a goodly share.

Garnett Ann Schultz

The Greatest Gift

Do you ever think you walk alone
And find it doesn't seem to end?
The gloomy days grow longer
And it seems you have no friends?

Do you ever sit and wait
For the telephone to ring?
And hasten to the mailbox
To see what the postman brings?

Arise, my friend, and telephone
Another in your town,
Write a cheery note or two,
Look up instead of down.

Hurry now and get a start,
Waste not another minute,
Life is surely worth the living
If you put something in it.

There is an old saying
That is often tried and true -
Do not ask, "What can I get?"
But, "What can I do for you?"

Mildred H. Bell

Reflections

If hearts were a little more caring
And eyes were a little less blind,
We might see, through the magic of sharing,
How easy it is to be kind.

If minds were a bit more revealing
And hands were more willing to greet,
We might give to each other a feeling
Of friendship whenever we meet.

If we could tear down all those roadblocks
That separate races and creeds
We might free from doubt's rusty old padlocks
Our oneness in hopes and in needs.

If we would let tolerance guide us
Where ignorance has not let us go,
We might turn back the foes that divide us,
The evils that weaken us so.

Then somehow we might find that highway,
Fog-hid by our own foolish pride,
And, shoulder to shoulder, some bright day
March up it to God's love-lit side.

John C. Bonser

How To Be
an Angel

Do you want to be an angel?
Let me tell you how to start,
Plant a tiny mustard seed
of flowers in your heart.

They'll grow in great proportions
To the planting that you sow,
Water them with kindness
And all the faith you know.

Then, put your trust in God above
To show how much you care,
He'll send you untold blessings
And all your burdens share!

Kathryn Wiesenhoefer

Help Me,
Lord!

When my little boat is sinking,
And the shore is not in sight,
And I have two broken paddles
To contribute to my plight,
It is not the time for weeping,
Though it surely crossed my mind,
What is needed here is action,
Of the very quickest kind.

So I called out, never thinking
Just what I was about,
"Lord please bail out this
little boat,
...I almost am without!"

Grace E. Easley

Whose Name
I'll Call

I know I'll stumble, I know I'll fall;
but I also know Whose Name I'll call.
And He will lift me to my feet,
and help me through the trials I meet.
He'll lift the burdens from my back,
and guide me onto life's "right track."
He'll make me feel so good inside,
when He reminds me why He died.
And why from death He rose again,
to wash me clean of all my sin.
So when you stumble, when you fall;
Jesus is the name to call,
And He will answer to your need,
if for forgiveness you will plead.

George A. Hellard Jr.

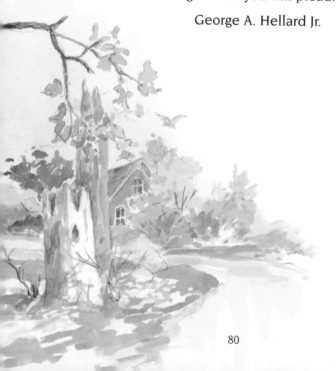

A Place We Share

My haven for heartaches, sorrows and griefs
Is a place I share with you -
Though we may be ages and miles apart -
We share a common pew -
For pains of my heart are no different than yours
I cry - and we suffer the same -
And the place where I pray for peace and relief
Is the same where you pray, in your name.

It's a place of salvation that both of us share -
In moments of trial or despair -
And the pleas that we whisper, for God to endear,
Are the pleas of a common prayer.
So - though we are ages and miles apart -
We are one, in His love and embrace,
Whenever we kneel - Wherever we kneel -
To pray for His comforts and Grace.

Michael Dubina

Beside Still Waters

Beside still waters may you rest
Secure as a bird within its nest.
Listen, friend, perhaps you'll hear
"The still small voice" that's always near.

Relax and set your spirit free;
Explore the fields of memory
And soar like an eagle high above
Remembering the ones you love.

Hear the babble of the brook,
And read again some cherished book.
Renew your faith, and spirit, too,
And walk barefoot in morning dew.

Watch the sun set on the shore...
These simple things we can't ignore.
Beside still waters may you find
Rest that comes with peace of mind.

Clay Harrison

...He leads me
beside still waters.
Ps. 23:2

Lonely Places

Often there are times in life
We need to be alone
To pray and find that inner strength
That God would make our own.

We need to seek a lonely place
To speak to God at will,
Where only in this solitude
Our minds and hearts are still.

And sometimes it is humbling, when
We seek a safe domain -
For needing lonely places, where
There's solace from our pain.

But oh, those tender moments
When we draw ourselves apart,
And find in lonely places...
God has healing for the heart.

Sister Miriam Barker, C.D.S.

*He restores
my soul.*
Ps. 23:3

There is beauty in the forest
When the trees are green and fair,
There is beauty in the meadow
When wild flowers scent the air.
There is beauty in the sunlight
And the soft blue beams above.
Oh, the world is full of beauty
When the heart is full of love.

A Season of Change

With awe I stand and welcome
November's mystic skies;
and its multi-textured canvas
that is crowded with surprise.
The harvest has been gathered,
fresh cider, too, is pressed,
silence reigns across the vales
and fields have earned their rest.
How classic are the orchards,
with their branch without its leaf;
and vines of twisted starkness,
of their burdens now relieved.

The pines, I know, are anxious;
their droll bleakness tells me so,
impatient for warm blankets
pieced with fleecy flakes of snow.
While the hills appear despairing,
now unshrouded of their grass;
and yet with hopeful voice proclaim,
"We know this, too, shall pass."
For now the winter's frosty wings
are swiftly flying near
and with the coming season
flows new music to my ear.
So to each season's symphony
I bid farewell and yearn
to greet each new performance
in its fanciful return.

Don Beckman

A True Friend

Time can hang so heavy
On a heart that's filled with grief,
The days go by so slowly,
And the night brings no relief.

"How can I face another day,"
I've heard so many say.
The answer lies within us,
We must kneel to God and pray.

We must ask our Lord to help us,
And to lift this load we bear.
There is nothing He can't render,
If we come to Him in prayer.

Oh, my friends, do not forsake Him
When your burdens weigh you down,
Though you look the wide world over,
No friend truer can be found.

Albert N. Theel

In Need

I need His grace to take my thoughts
From worldly things I love
And set my heart on lasting gifts -
The treasures from above.

The precious peace and love and joy
That only He can give
I need to value more each day,
The longer that I live.

Through every day I need His help -
Temptations wait for me -
If I am going to become
The one I ought to be.

Rachel Hartnett

God's Hand

When Jack Frost dips his frosty toe
Into the greenery below,
'Tis when all of nature bow their heads
In pots, on hills and flower beds.

As if God waved a lofty hand
And changed the color of the land,
But we again will see His power
Through winter as we count each hour.

Soon, the peeking sun will bring
A warmer sun, that sign of spring,
And as this season comes along
'Tis like an old familiar song.

It is as if all souls realize
Each day we're here is a special prize.
And as time grows, we understand
The magic love of our Father's hand.

James Joseph Huesgen

Peace

My home is never empty,
Although I be alone
I hear the voices of angels
To God, - their love intone!

I feel His very presence
In wind and storm or rain
That beats upon my window
And quiets all my pain!

I see His face in every nook
each cranny of my room
I know He's ever near to me
To chase away - my "secret gloom."

I'm sure He'll never leave me,
His promise He'll fulfill
To keep me close - In home and heart
And softly whisper "Peace - Be Still."

Kathryn Wiesenhoefer

Oh, Maker of Beauty

Tonight as I look
Toward the heavens above,
I see in the moonbeam
A wonder of love.
It seems to be saying
I've traveled and far,
Yet I stay in the presence
Of the lone evening star.
This lovely old moonbeam
Has kept company,
Shined down from the heavens
For the world all to see.

And if one should be looking
Toward the east or the west,
To the north or the south
You can still see it best.
Oh, Maker of moonbeams
And starshine of love,
Designer of earth
And of heaven above,
Oh, Artist of beauty
You give and for free,
Your wonders of glory
For the world all to see.

Katherine Smith Matheney

Life's Race

Life is a long cross-country race
Where Christ Our Lord once set the pace,
And taught us how "Life's Race" is run -
Not only run, but truly won.
He taught us of His Father's Love
Which floweth freely from above.
By His example He did show
The way to live and the way to go.
And, yet, how maudlin is the mind
That ever seeks yet seldom finds,
That "Strait and Narrow Course" to run,
Where life eternal may be won.

Yes! Life indeed, is like a race
Where thy own conscience sets the pace,
So let thy conscience be thy wealth,
And "Love thy neighbor as thyself!"
Oh, Love! How wonderful this word!
How sweet it rings when often heard!
Its truth is found in God above,
For Love is God, and God is Love!
Now, tired runner, slow thy pace,
For Christ has won Salvation's Grace.
Yet let it not be said of me,
That Christ once died quite needlessly.

Clayton G. Moseley

Gentle Jesus

Gentle Jesus listen closely
To the words that I would say,
'Tis with love that knows no limits,
That I come to Thee today.

For without You life is empty,
With no comfort anyplace,
I have naught save You to help me,
Do not turn away Thy face.

Gentle Jesus teach me patience,
Take away this foolish pride,
Grant I only be permitted,
To continue at Thy side.

Though my heart is sometimes weary,
And my eyes are filled with tears,
I have only but to tell Thee
And my sorrow disappears.

Gentle Jesus, Lord and Master,
Deep within this human shell,
Lives a soul which Thou hast ransomed,
It would love Thee long and well.

You have felt as I am feeling,
Who could better understand,
Than the One who meekly listened,
To their "crucify the Man!"

Grace E. Easley

$\mathcal{B}$e like the bird that,
pausing in her flight awhile
on boughs too slight,
Feels them give way
beneath her and yet sings,
Knowing that she hath wings.

Victor Hugo

Then Sings My Soul!

We take for granted many things
in the passing of a day
Like hummingbirds with tiny wings,
and moonlight on the bay.
We fail to hear the robin's song
when Spring is in the air
Annoyed that Winter was too long
and all the trees are bare.

How often do we fail to see
the rainbows high above
Which come and go as silently
as feathers from a dove.
Summers pass and crimson leaves
fall gently at our door
When Autumn wears her golden sleeves
on nature's ballroom floor.

Beneath the sea the coral reefs
attract the diver's eye
For beauty there beyond belief
lies hidden from the sky.
The things of God are everywhere
the human eye can see -
Then sings my soul in joyful prayer
for all His majesty!

Clay Harrison

Precious Windows

When I think of windows
this thought comes to me,
"I own precious windows...
My eyes, that can see."

They grasp for all beauty.
They labor in sight.
They whisper in darkness,
Acknowledge delight.

When I think of windows
I give thought to mine.
God gifted me two eyes
Each healthy and fine.

I hope most sincerely
I never abuse
This privilege of "seeing"
God gave me to use!

Tee Lowrey

A Prayer

Let the lowliest task be mine,
Grateful, so the work be Thine;
Let me find the humblest place
In the shadow of Thy grace;
Blest to me were any spot
Where temptation whispers not.
If there be some weaker one,
Give me strength to help him on;
If a blinder soul there be,
Let me guide him nearer Thee.

Make my mortal dreams come true
With the work I fain would do;
Clothe with life the weak intent,
Let me be the thing I meant;
Let me find in Thy employ
Peace that dearer is than joy.
Out of self to love be led,
And to heaven acclimated,
Until all things sweet and good
Seem my natural habitude.

John Greenleaf Whittier

*As God's chosen ones,
holy and beloved,
clothe yourselves with compassion,
kindness, humility, meekness
and patience.*
Col. 3:12

The Season of
the Roadside Stand

It's the season of the roadside stand,
And along the country roads
We see displayed the harvest yield
From seed which the tiller sowed.

There are golden ears of sweet corn,
Gourds of every size;
Beans, both green and yellow;
Potatoes, red and white.

There are solid heads of cabbage,
Some moss-curled parsley, green;
Tomatoes, squash, and pumpkins...
What a thankful autumn scene!

It's the season of the roadside stand;
How the merchants' faces beam
As they strive to please each buyer
Of this produce, freshly gleaned.

Loise Pinkerton Fritz

*Thou crownest the year
with thy goodness;
and thy paths
drop fatness.*
Ps. 65:11

98

In the Arms
of Jesus

In the holy arms of Jesus
There is haven from our fears
And a refuge for the heartaches
That engulf a life in tears
For He loves us, with devotion,
Through all phases of our life -
Though we, oftentimes, deny Him
In our miseries of strife.

He is caring and forgiving
Of our frailties of heart
And the sins of human weakness
We commission and impart,
But His arms are always open -
To endear us in embrace -
When we pray to Him for refuge
and the comforts of His Grace.

Michael Dubina

Sweet Bye and Bye

The rickety old barn by the side of the road
Is wrinkled and stooped from its past heavy load.

The pigeons and swallows still nest in its hair -
That its life is near spent, they seem unaware.

It sways in the wind as it leans on its cane
Oblivious to storm clouds and forthcoming rain.

It's like that with many I meet on the street -
They seem not to notice the ripening wheat

Or that angels are waiting with sickles in hand
To harvest the grain at our Savior's command.

So let us put on that garment of white
Lest Jesus should come like a thief in the night.

And let us be ready to meet in the sky
Forever to dwell in the "Sweet Bye and Bye."

Luther Elvis Albright

To Love the Earth

To love the earth means oh so much
To grasp the soil with gentle touch,
And feel it there within your hand
The beauty of God's wondrous land,
To plant and sow each tiny seed
Eliminate the growing weed.

A gentle man will work the fields
And treasure crops the good earth yields,
To nurture plants and watch them grow
Delight to see them, row on row,
Such happiness then fills his soul
To reach his ever sought for goal.

To reap the harvest of his toil
From out the magic of the soil,
A partner to God high above
He cultivates in hope and love,
Delights to nature's lasting worth
A wisdom real - to love the earth.

Garnett Ann Schultz

The Ministry
of Kindness

Lord, my ministry is kindness,
Loving thoughts and words and deeds,
I dedicate my life to You
To serve my neighbor's needs;
One may need loving assistance,
One, just a call to keep in touch,
And one may need a word of praise
That says, "I love you very much."
To one I'll give material gifts
To another, gifts divine
But to You, Lord, I'll give myself
To be forever Thine.

Sister Mary Gemma Brunke,S.C.

*...by love
serve one another.*
Gala. 5:13

My God Is
in Control!

When worries seem to overcome,
And tension fills my soul,
My God is just a prayer away,
I know He's in control.

When burdens seem so hard to bear,
And triumphs seem so few,
That's when He takes my hand once more,
To lead me right on through.

God has a reason for each trial,
And as my life unfolds,
He knows the things I can't explain,
And what my future holds.

O'er mountains or through valleys,
I have learned to be content,
I know He'll work things out to be
The way that they were meant.

May I be strengthened by each trial,
May I, His name extoll,
And never should I once forget,
That God is in control!

Carol McKenney

Use Me Lord

Use me Lord and let me serve
In every way I can.
Let me channel love and hope,
According to your plan.
Show me the way, lead me to where
There is a plea for help and care.
Then let me be the light, and means
To be the answer to a prayer.
Use my talents and my strengths
That I might serve You best
By sharing all You've given me,
For which I'm truly blessed.
Use me Lord, give me the words
To comfort and console.
Then guide me with each step I take
To touch the heart of some dear soul.
For I have much that I can give
And I offer willingly
To be Your vessel while I serve,
Dear Precious Lord, use me.

Patience Allison Hartbauer

For All to Share

I thank God for the many things
He often sends my way,
The love and peace that I enjoy
Which often fill my day.

These lovely gifts He gives to me
But I must prove my worth,
If Paradise I hope to see
When I have left this earth.

Thus I must lend a helping hand
To those who are in need
And find the lost and floundering souls
Who need someone to lead -

Give freely of my time to those
Who sorrow and despair
And hold the hands of those in pain
And show them that I care.

The love and peace that I enjoy
Is there for all to share,
If you desire these gifts from God
Just go to Him in prayer.

Dolores Karides

Perennial Perfection

Child, you're a flower
Flourished from a seed
Nurtured, loved, protected
Perfect, yes indeed.

Child you're a flower,
Skin of velvet rose,
Scent of fields of lilacs,
Dainty hands and toes.

Child, you're a flower,
Finer by the day,
Growing strong and handsome
In your special way.

Child, you're a flower,
A gift of true delight,
Heaven knows I'm thankful
Every day and night.

Janice Cortis Kasowski

*"...Let the children
come to me and
do not prevent them;
for the Kingdom of God
belongs to such as these."*
Luke 18:16

The Love
of a Child

There's nothing as lovely and nothing as true
As the love of a child in our care,
Nothing as sweet as the soft wistful eyes
Or the arms they so willingly share.

There's sweetness and joy such as none we have known,
There's tenderness, warmth and delight,
So wondrously rare is the mind of a child,
A portion of wisdom and light.

The love of a child is a treasure to keep,
Do nurture it day unto day,
This sweet little soul God has placed in your care
To guide it and show it the way.

It will blossom and bloom as the days shall unfold,
You will know that on you God has smiled,
For nothing's more precious or more to be sought
Than the heart and the love of a child.

Garnett Ann Schultz

"Amen, I say to you,
whoever does not accept the
Kingdom of God like a child
will not enter it."
Luke 18:17

Blessings
Counted...

...For sunshine, for quenching rain,
For relief of our pain.

...For green leaves on trees so tall.
For Winter, Spring, Summer and Fall.

...For midnight, for afternoon,
For starlight and for the moon.

...For laughter,
For children's smiles,
For walking with us across the miles.

...For tears of joy, for hearts that care.
For the ability to love,
For the ability to share.

For gentle guidance,
For constant love,
We owe our thanks to God above.

Marsha Smith Meigs

When you hearken
to the voice of the Lord, your God,
all these blessings will come upon you
and overwhelm you.
Deut. 28:2

Spring's Arrival

I didn't hear a bugle blow
When spring arrived today,
Nor did I hear the whole world shout
Along the springtide way.
Instead I heard the trilling sound
Of songbirds everywhere,
The gentle breezes, humming bees,
The wild geese in the air.

I didn't see a big fanfare
When spring came by our way,
Nor did I see a festive feast
To mark this gladsome day.
Instead I saw rebirth of life,
A world of blossoming;
Oh, yes, I saw the power of God
In this first day of spring.

Loise Pinkerton Fritz

*And he changeth
the times and
the seasons.*
Daniel 2:21

In His Hand

My Father sees inside my heart,
He knows my every need.
His plan for me He will reveal,
If on His Word I'll feed.

He spoke the universe in place;
He's Master of the sea.
When storms of life are raging,
I know He'll pilot me.

Why should I worry then, or fret?
For God, who gave His Son,
Holds all my moments in His hand
And gives them one by one.

Shirley W. Langley

*In the shadow
of His hand
hath He hid me....*
Is. 49:2

I Know God's Love
Is Everywhere

I know God's love is everywhere,
In the beauty of the land,
It's as clean as the shells along the shore
After the waves have washed the sand.
It's a contented peace that you can feel
Just as twilight blankets the earth,
As fresh as the morning dew on the rose
When night to the dawn gives birth.
It's the gentle patter of the rain
After a long hot summer's day,
A radiant light that forever glows
When storm clouds roll our way.
It's as gold as the leaves when
they begin to change,
As brisk as an autumn morn,
As soft as the snowflakes that kiss your cheek
When a winter's day is born.
It sparkles as bright as jewels in the snow,
When the moon sheds its silvery light,
It outnumbers the stars in the heavens above
On a clear crisp winter's night.
For nature sings God's song of love,
In the beauty of the land,
We have only to listen with our hearts
To know God's love for man.

Debbie Hiber

I'd Like
To Share
My Dream

I'd like to share my dream with you
and tell you what is best to do,
So, first before you start the day,
ask God for courage as you pray.
Whatsoever things are lovely,
live them in your heart,
Whatsoever things are honest
never let them part.
Do not turn away discouraged -
keep your eyes upon your dream,
Fight the things within you, even
hopeless they may seem,
Keep going in one direction
laughing at your fate,

Turning to the things you dreamed of,
on the track of something great!
Fill your heart with rainbows,
don't let clouds linger there,
For there's no time for sadness
when happiness fills the air.
We all can't climb the mountain
to that glorious height,
But we can go on ahead and upward
to the Guiding Light.
Don't worry about the yesterdays -
the winds have blown away,
Lift up your heart and sing again
for there's another day.
So, if you let me share my dream,
life will feel sublime,
For somewhere just beyond the clouds
the sun will always shine.

Doris K. Finck

God Made
An Autumn Day

God spoke to Mother Nature
One bright October day,
Then handed her a paint brush
And colors bright and gay,
Was then she formed a sunrise
To touch the leaves of gold,
And blended bits of scarlet
All beautiful and bold.

At eventide, a sunset
Was added to it all,
The blue of sky - a gentle breeze
That bid the leaves to fall,
The magic of the hilltops
Each dream along the way,
God tucked away the summer
Then made an autumn day.

Garnett Ann Schultz

A Touch
of Autumn

A touch of Autumn fills the air
with great expectations everywhere.
Hot summer days and humid nights
have given way to cool delights.
The frosted pumpkins in the glen
have children wearing silly grins.
Our harvest dreams have been fulfilled,
now dreams of Christmas have us thrilled.

The stars seem brighter than before
like fireflies at Heaven's door.
Silver moonlight and Autumn breeze
have transformed the golden trees
into chapels made of light
singing praises throughout the night.
A touch of Autumn fills the air
with thoughts that God is always there!

Clay Harrison

Life's
Ultimate Goal

It takes a lot of courage,
And great determination,
To overcome the obstacles
And reach a destination!

To be endowed with patience
Takes more than self-control;
It takes a lot of praying
When striving for that goal.

The road was never easy
To glory or to fame,
For in this world of strangers,
You are just another name!

You must expect to struggle,
And take it on the chin.
There always is a battle,
Before someone can win.

You must not cry or falter,
For once the game's begun
You have to keep on pitching;
Don't quit until you've won.

And once you taste the glory,
Don't rest on laurels pay!
For fame is not decisive —
It, too, can fade away!

An honor is God's blessing
Enriching heart and soul;
It's when you uplift others,
You've reached life's highest goal.

Gene Appleby

Place Your Faith

Place your faith and trust in God
With each new dawning day,
And He will be your beacon bright
Each step along the way.

He always will forgive you
Through acts of sin and wrong,
And in your hour of weakness
Will help you to be strong.

He never will forsake you
As friends so often do,
But be your staunch companion
Day after day anew.

He always will sustain you
In time of great despair.
His love for you is timeless
And present everywhere.

Harold F. Mohn

*And again,
I will put
my trust
in Him...*
Heb. 2:13

I Trust Him Still

I trusted God when skies were bright,
And summer days were blue and gold,
When life held only joy-filled days
And happiness was mine to hold.

I trusted God when roses bloomed,
When autumn showed her lovely face,
But when the season passed, and all
Was stripped of beauty and of grace -

I found life's winter, too, was bleak.
My skies once blue now overcast.
Storm clouds were looming, and I asked -
"Can I trust now, as in the past?"

I trusted when the skies were bright,
And roses bloomed so sweet and fair.
How small my faith if now I ceased
To trust God's wisdom and His care.

I trust Him still. And when has passed
All heartache, and the winter's gloom,
I know I'll see, and love more dear,
A summer day when roses bloom.

Beverly J. Anderson

On a Winter Morning

I took a walk this morning,
I had to go and see,
The world of white that winter's hands,
Had fashioned just for me.

Alone beneath the somber skies,
I felt the silent spell,
And I beheld a fairyland,
As feathered snowflakes fell.

Across a little wooden bridge,
My footprints in the snow,
Left little tracks which clearly told
Which way I meant to go.

With eyes alight and cheeks aflame,
I climbed the nearest hill,
And on the threshold of such joy
My heart grew hushed and still.

The glistening white cathedral,
Of the forest towered high,
And I, a humble worshipper,
Sensed God was passing by!

I do not know what happened,
But I am not the same,
And I went home a better soul
...Than when I came!

Grace E. Easley

Lest I Forget, Lord

Lest I forget to thank You, Lord,
For all You've done for me,
Not only now, but every day,
Please "jog" my memory.
Lest I forget that in each life
Your children here below
Have some distress akin to mine..
All this, I need to know.
Fill me with Your compassion
And a love for everyone..
To overlook the faults in them
And see the good they've done.
For I am weak just like the rest
And need Your saving grace,
The glory of eternity
Will be to see Your face!
I must be sure I've done my best..
God, help me as I try.
We only have one life to live..
There is a time to die.

Gene Appleby

My Guiding Light

Illuminator of my soul,
Shine bright for me today -
Push back the shadows from my path
Till I can see the way
That You would have me go, dear God,
- Don't let me blindly grope -
Let Your Holiness surround me
And, too, Your blessed Hope.
Grant me wisdom and discernment
- Bathe my spirit in Light!
Remove from me those obstacles
That so obscure my sight.
And when the way ahead is clear
Please take me by the hand -
For if I try to walk alone,
I'll step in sinking sand.
Dear Jesus, Lover of my soul,
You know what's best for me -
And if I stay within Your Light,
That plan You'll let me see.
So grasp my hand and hold it tight,
Lest I begin to stray -
And be my ever Guiding Light
...Beginning with today.

Denise A. DeWald

"... I am the light of the world.
Whoever follows me will never walk in darkness,
but will have the light of life."
John 8:12

Someone Shares Our Burdens

Have you ever known days when nothing goes right,
When everything seems to go wrong?
Have you ever had times when friends let you down
And you're weak when you want to be strong?

Have problems beset you on every side,
'Til you simply don't know where to turn,
And no one seems able to lend you a hand
When you seek a solution to learn?

Has illness or grief taken over your life?
Is your body or mind wracked with pain?
Are you so filled with spite, guilt, envy or hate
That happy thoughts cannot remain?

We will all suffer anguish sometime in our life,
But we don't have to face it alone;
There is Someone who's waiting our burdens to share,
There is Someone who'll make them His Own.

That Someone is Jesus, through Him is the Way
That leads to contentment and rest;
He'll give us the strength all our trials to endure...
In His love all our days will be blessed.

So turn to the Master, with prayers and praise,
Give yourself to Him body and soul;
In that glorious bondage you'll find yourself free
To live with His throne as your goal.

Alice J. Christianson

Be Not Dismayed
By Dismal Days

It's a dismal, dreary morning and as I sometimes do
I feel a little dreary and kinda downcast, too,
For let nobody tell you that life's a "happy song"
And that we just keep smiling
when everything goes wrong...
For it just would not be natural to always wear a smile,
For a smile would be a "silly grin" if it covered up a trial...
For there are certain periods when the soul is "sweetly sad"
As it contemplates the mystery
of both good times and bad...
We're not really discontented and we are never unaware
That the Good Lord up in heaven
has us always in His care,
But the soul of man is restless
and it just keeps longing for
A haven that is safe and sure that will last forevermore...
And as I sit here writing this
a thought passed through my mind -
"Why dwell on past or future
or what's ahead or gone behind?"
Just follow God unquestioningly
because you love Him so,
For if you trust His judgment
there is nothing you need know!

Helen Steiner Rice

The Source and
Father of Mercies

When trials of life are hard-pressing,
Oh, turn to the Lord, for He sees.
He's the Source and the Father of mercies;
Too, the God of all comfort is He.

No matter how great is the trial,
Still greater His mercy and grace.
He'll not test us more than we're able
But will give us a way of escape.

In sufferings and all tribulations,
He lovingly comforts His own
That we might in turn comfort others,
Their troubled hearts gently console.

So when trials so greatly assail us,
No trust should we put in ourselves.
The Source and the Father of mercies
Will all our anxieties quell.

Loise Pinkerton Fritz

Blessed be God, even the Father of
our Lord Jesus Christ, the Father of mercies,
and the God of all comfort.
2 Cor. 1:3

I've Burned
a Lot of Bridges
in My Time

I've burned a lot of bridges in my time,
Left a trail of ashes through the years,
Backed myself into a solid wall,
And been to blame for more than half my tears.
Tripped on pride and fell upon my face,
Bitten off much more than I could chew,
Detoured over many needless miles,
And even missed the boat a time or two.

"Walking in where angels fear to tread,"
I spoke my mind more often than I should,
Sinner...Saint...a name is but a name,
For I was sometimes bad and sometimes good.
A loner more by choice than circumstance,
I shunned the crowds to mingle with my kind,
Finding much of beauty even though
...I've burned a lot of bridges in my time.

Grace E. Easley

Seasons of the Heart

I linger by my window pane
Where Summer memories remain,
And high above the fallen snow
Bright silken flowers seem to grow.

I reminisce of Spring's sweet song
And for her vibrant beauty long,
I miss the fragrance of the rose
And velvet grass between my toes.

But soon I'll hear the songbird's trill
For it has always been God's Will
That Winter shall give way to Spring
And all the joys that it can bring.

Catherine Janssen Irwin